FIDEL CASTRO

Communist Dictator of Cuba

BY GERALD KURLAND

B. A. Long Island University
M. A. Brooklyn College
Ph. D. The City University of New York

SamHar Press
Division of Story House Corp.

D. Steve Rahmas, *A. B., J. D., Columbia U., Editor*

Compiled with the assistance of the Research Staff
of SamHar Press.

SamHar Press
Charlotteville, N.Y.   12036
A Division of Story House Corp.
1972

92
CAS

Kurland, Dr. Gerald
    Fidel Castro, Communist Dictator of Cuba. Charlotteville,
N.Y., Story House Corp. (SamHar Press), 1972.

    32 p. 22 cm. (Outstanding Personalities, no. 36)
    Bibliography: p. 32
    Story House Prebound

    1. Castro, Fidel 1927— 2. Cuba—History—1959 (Series:
Outstanding Personalities)

F1788.K8   923.2

(The above card has been cataloged by the editor and may not be
identical to that of Library of Congress. Library card portrayed above
is 80% of original size.)

Preassigned Library of Congress Catalog Card Number: 72-75370

FIDEL CASTRO

Communist Dictator of Cuba

At 2 A.M. on the morning of January 1, 1959, Fulgencio Batista, the hated military dictator of Cuba, fled the Presidential Palace at Havana and went into exile in the Dominican Republic. Only a few days before, Santa Clara had fallen to the Rebel Army of Fidel Castro, and Batista, realizing that his disheartened army was on the verge of collapse, decided to leave Cuba while he could still enjoy the millions of dollars of public moneys which he had illicitly placed in foreign banks. In a triumphal week-long procession, Fidel Castro emerged from his stronghold in the Sierra Maestra Mountains and journeyed to Havana. Whereever he went in Cuba, he was hailed as a liberator, and he constantly reiterated his pledge to establish a democratic society for all the Cuban people. In the United States, as in Cuba, Fidel Castro was also hailed as a liberator and as a champion of democratic freedom. In April, 1959, Castro went to the United States to address the American Society of Newspaper Editors, and his trip was a complete triumph.

THE GREAT BETRAYAL "We want to establish in Cuba a true democracy," Castro told the American editors, "without any trace of Fascism, Peronism, or Communism. We are against every kind of totalitarianism." Later, on a nationwide television news interview program, the Cuban leader flatly stated, "I am not a Communist, nor do I agree with Communism." The American people and their government were only too willing to take Castro at his word, and during this honeymoon period in United States-Cuban relations, the

3

entire American people wished the Cuban revolution well. Yet, within two years, the United States would break diplomatic relations with Castro's Cuba and would actively encourage the ill-fated Bay of Pigs expedition designed to topple his dictatorship. This lamentable state of affairs came about because Fidel Castro betrayed his own revolution and committed the supreme infanticide by killing the democratic promise which he himself had made. Instead of creating a democratic society in Cuba, Castro took the Cuban people down the path of Communist dictatorship and established a police state tyranny every bit as bad as the Batista dictatorship which he overthrew. The reasons for this betrayal of the Cuban revolution are not fully known and are not likely to be known for some time, but a large part of the answer may be found in the character and psychological make-up of Fidel Castro.

THE YOUNG FIDEL Until the time that he led the attack on the Moncada Barracks in July, 1953, Fidel Castro's life is a puzzle wrapped inside an enigma. Accounts of his pre-1953 activities are so contradictory that the biographer is at a loss to distinguish fact from fancy. Castro himself has prepared a lengthy autobiography which will probably not be published during his lifetime. The autobiography will, of course, clear up a good deal of the mystery surrounding his career, but like other Communist leaders Castro is not anxious to set the historical record straight. The mystery shrouding his past adds to his charisma and personal magnetism and permits him to alter the details of his past career to fit the ideological party line of the moment. We do know, however, that his father Angel Castro came to Cuba from Spain as a poor agricultural laborer. By dint of hard work and intelligent management, Angel became a farmer, prospered, and added to his landholdings. Eventually, he became a *latifundista* (plantation owner) and controlled 23,300 acres of choice sugar lands. His plantation was near Biran, on the north coast of Oriente province, and Angel was among the wealthiest planters in the province. After the death of his wife (who had given him two children), Angel took Lina Gonzalez, a Cuban creole who was a household servant in his employ, as his mistress. Lina gave Angel another seven children, and shortly after the birth of her fourth child, Fidel, Angel agreed to marry her. Fidel Castro was born on his father's sugar plantation on August 13, 1926, and was fortunate enough to escape the grinding poverty which afflicted the vast majority of the Cuban people. We know little of his childhood except that he intensely disliked his father, but was very close to his mother. His defenders allege that his dislike of his father stemmed from his outrage at the way Angel exploited and brutalized the peasants who worked his lands. However, this sounds like a later rationalization and should not be accepted at face value. EDUCATION Again, according to Fidel's friends, when he was six or seven years old, he asked Angel to send him to school. The father, however, had a low opinion of education and refused, whereupon Fidel threatened to burn down the family's home if his father did not give in to his demand. Strong willed and bellicose, Fidel convinced his father that he meant what he said, and rather than risk the safety of his home, Angel agreed to send his son to a Jesuit primary school in Santiago de Cuba. Fidel stayed at the home of his godparents, who apparently treated him rather harshly and barely gave him enough food to sustain life. This privation, though, did not diminish his warlike spirit one whit. At school, Fidel became involved in a quarrel with a much older boy and got into a fight which he could not possibly win. He took a beating that day, but rather than concede defeat, he kept picking fights with the older boy and kept getting beaten until his bigger opponent tired of the one-sided fight and let him have his way. Fidel has never accepted the "if you can't beat them, join them" philosophy. If he cannot beat an opponent, he lets the opponent beat him until he grows tired, and then he takes over. It is this fighting spirit which explains his bellicosity towards the United States. In any event, in 1942, having graduated from the primary school in Santiago, Fidel was sent to the Colegio Belen, a Jesuit preparatory school in Havana.

Apparently he was sent there at his mother's insistence, for with his father's attitude toward education, it is unlikely that Angel would have voluntarily sent his son to a college preparatory school. From the conflicting accounts which can be pieced together, it would appear that Fidel was a better than average student; his best subjects were history, Spanish, and agriculture. He participated in a wide variety of sports and, in 1944, was voted the school's best athlete. Determined to pursue a career in law, Fidel Castro, after his graduation from the Colegio Belen, entered the University of Havana's School of Law in the fall of 1945. Castro's years at the University of Havana is the most disputed and mysterious period of his life.

"GANGSTER" In later years, Castro claimed that he discovered Marxism-Leninism while a student at the University of Havana, and that his reading of Communist writers slowly turned him into a Marxist-Leninist. However, Herbert L. Matthews, his most knowledgeable biographer, disputes this contention and denies that Castro had anything more than a nodding acquaintance of Marxism while at the University of Havana. Indeed, it would appear that Castro had precious little time for study. Throughout his university career, Fidel Castro carried a revolver with him - and he had need of it. He quickly joined the Union Insurreccional Revolucionaria (UIR), which was a terroristic group dedicated to the overthrow of the corrupt militarists and industrialists who ruled Cuba. Ideologically, the UIR's program was vague, but it does not appear to have been a Communist dominated organization. Most of its energies were absorbed in fighting the Movimiento Socialista Revolucionaria (MSR) which was a rival gang of student terrorists. No less than four students were murdered in strife between the UIR and the MSR while Castro was attending the university, and his enemies claim that he personally murdered a number of those students. However, no documentary evidence has yet turned up to verify that accusation. Contemporary intelligence reports commissioned by the United States government did label Fidel Castro a "gangster" and as a man to be watched. The label

6

was, indeed, accurate.

REVOLUTIONARY In 1947, Castro and a number of his fellow students became involved in a plot to over-throw General Trujillo, the dictator of the Dominican Republic. The plan called for the students to acquire arms and a yacht, sail to the Dominican Republic, es-tablish a beachhead, and arouse the local populace to join their rebellion. It was, in short, the type of comic-opera militarism which delights the Latin American temperament. Unfortunately for the students, United States intelligence agents got wind of the plot, informed the Cuban government, and Cuban patrol boats inter-cepted the yacht as it was about to leave Cuban waters. To avoid being captured, Fidel Castro jumped over-board and swam to shore dragging his submachine gun behind him. He managed to elude the Cuban police, and in April, 1948, turned up in Bogata, Colombia, as the representative of the University of Havana at a Latin American student conference. While the conference was in session, Bogata's university students went on a rampage hoping to topple the Colombian government. Castro actively participated in the student riots, and, according to his enemies, he was personally respon-sible for the murder of at least one and possibly six Roman Catholic priests. His partisans have vehemently denied the charge, and existing documentation is not sufficient to prove the accusation true. In any event, the student uprising failed to topple the Colombian government, and Fidel Castro managed to make a safe exit from the country and return to Havana. There, in July, 1948, he was arrested and charged with the murder of a police sergeant during a student distur-bance at the university. The charges against him had to be dropped when his accusers mysteriously changed their story and refused to identify him as the killer. Castro asserts that the murder charge was a frame-up, but his activities at the university reveal him to have been an anarchist who sought violence for its own sake. He believed in nothing, but wanted to destroy his existing society for the sheer pleasure of seeing it destroyed. Like the modern student left, he sought only the gratification of his hate-filled passions and

7

used the existence of social injustice to justify the anti-social acts of violence in which he indulged. MARRIAGE AND CAREER While at the University of Havana, Castro fell in love with a fellow student, Mirta Diaz-Balart, whom he married over the strenuous objections of her parents who refused to approve or recognize the marriage. After honeymooning in Miami, the couple returned to Havana, where Castro completed his education. School records indicate that he received excellent grades, but Latin American universities are notorious for student intimidation of the faculty, and "gangsters" always receive high grades. On September 1, 1949, Mirta gave birth to a son, Fidelito, and Castro was about to embark upon his legal career.

INTERLUDE We know next to nothing of Fidel Castro's activities from 1950 to 1952. Ostensibly, he was in private law practice, but he never earned much at his practice. According to his admirers, Castro was not a financial success because he defended clients who were too poor to pay him and who lacked political connections. According to his opponents, Castro failed to develop a successful practice because he was an incompetent attorney and was constantly preoccupied with political intrigues. Sometime during this period, he joined the Ortodoxo party (Party of the Cuban people), which was organized back in 1946 to press for land reform, regulation of the great industries, and the implementation of a true political democracy. In 1952 Fidel Castro became an Ortodoxo party candidate for the Cuban congress and was confident that he would win the June election. However, before the Cuban people even had a chance to vote, Fulgencio Batista staged a *coup d'etat* on March 10, 1952, and seized control of the government. Batista proceeded to establish one of the most brutal dictatorships in Cuban history, and Fidel Castro, who lusted for power for himself, was able to capitalize on the genuine frustrations of the Cuban people and topple the Batista dictatorship. However, before the Castro revolution can be understood, it is necessary to relate something of the history of Cuba.

FRUSTRATED NATIONALISM Cuba, the Pearl of the Antilles, is an island of fabulous wealth, but yet the Cuban people are poor. Cuba's rich soil yields sugar and tobacco whose quality can be equalled nowhere else, and the island is rich in mineral wealth, especially in nickel. Unfortunately, the Spanish conquistadores who took over the island soon after the voyage of Christopher Columbus were a brutal lot interested only in economic exploitation. They enslaved the local Indian population and literally worked them to death. When the Indians were on the verge of becoming extinct, Negro slaves were imported from Africa to take their places on the plantations and in the mines. As Cuba developed, the Spanish upper-class led a life of indolent luxury, but for the Indian, Negro, and mestizo (persons of mixed Spanish-Indian-Negro blood) masses, Cuba was a house of bondage which knew only misery, grinding poverty, and early death from deprivation and overwork. In 1868 Cuban nationalists rebelled and began a ten year guerrilla war which failed to oust the Spaniards. In 1895 the brilliant Jose Marti (whose disciple Castro claims to be) took over leadership of the nationalist movement and resumed the civil war. Marti was killed in a Spanish ambush in 1895, but the revolution did not die with him. Instead it gathered momentum, and with the intervention of the United States of America in 1898 Cuba was finally able to throw off the tyrannous yoke of Spain. It is estimated that in the thirty years from 1868-1898 four hundred thousand Cuban men, women, and children died in the struggle against Spanish rule. But instead of achieving national independence, the Cuban people discovered that they had thrown out the Spaniards only to become a protectorate and virtual colony of the United States.

YANKEE IMPERIALISM From 1898-1902 Cuba was under the direct military occupation of the United States. Indeed, American occupation was necessary during the period of transition from Spanish rule to the creation of a national Cuban government, and the Americans made significant contributions to the improvement of Cuba's health, educational, and transportation services. Had it not been for the Platt amendment, the

American occupation would have left no bitterness. However, at American insistence, the Cubans were forced to write into their constitution a clause empowering the United States to militarily intervene into the internal affairs of Cuba whenever the United States judged that democratic government was in danger of being overthrown. The Platt amendment was a national humiliation which the Cubans have never forgotten or forgiven. Although the United States renounced its Platt amendment rights in 1934, it intervened in Cuban affairs on numerous occasions before that date, and even after our renunciation the American ambassador in Havana continued to issue orders to the Cuban president and to treat him like an office boy. While the United States gave up its Platt amendment rights, it did not renounce its economic domination of Cuba. When Fidel Castro came to power in 1959, the United States had investments in Cuba totaling $800-900 million, and American corporations controlled 90% of the island's electric and telephone service, 50% of the railroad system, 40% of the sugar acreage, and 25% of the banking industry. Many Cubans felt that their national wealth was being drained off by United States business interests, and they were resentful of our interference in their affairs and our support of their military masters. Cuban nationalists did not feel that they were truly independent, they believed that Cuba was a colony of the United States, and they harbored deep-seated hostility against Yankee imperialism. It was Fidel Castro's genius to be able to tap this anti-Americanism and to make it serve his regime.

NATIONAL CORRUPTION Perhaps United States domination of Cuba's government and economy would not have rankled so much had Cuba's leaders been honestly dedicated to improving the life of the common people. Unfortunately, from 1903 to 1959 dictator followed dictator in a seemingly endless procession. Practically every high official of the Cuban government used his position for personal enrichment. So many people stole public funds, so many officials had secret bank accounts in foreign countries, that the corruption of the Cuban government became a continuous national disgrace. The 100 powerful families who owned 20% of Cuba's landed wealth allied themselves with corrupt military leaders in order to keep the masses in poverty and to strike down any civil leader who dared to talk about social reform or economic justice. And to add to the insult of it all, the United States, the world's leading champion of democracy, invariably supported the military dictators. That the Cuban people should embrace a leader who promised democracy and social justice is not surprising; that Fidel Castro betrayed his promise will redound to his everlasting discredit.

BATISTA Fulgencio Batista was another in the long line of military dictators who had ruled Cuba. Back in 1933 he was a young colonel who had helped to topple the dictatorship of Gerardo Machado. Rising rapidly in the ranks of the army, Batista became chief of staff of the Cuban army, and, in 1940, he became president of the republic. When his term as president expired in 1944, Batista left office and went into wealthy retirement in Florida. However, he continued to play a behind-the-scenes role in the Cuban government, and after being succeeded by two inept presidents, he decided to take power in March, 1952. This time, though, his regime reached new heights of repression and corruption. The secret police freely used torture to break down and extract confessions from suspected revolutionaries and subversives; North American gangsters infiltrated the gambling casinos of Havana; public officials profited from organized vice; and the leaders of the Cuban labor movement openly conspired with industrialists to stifle the legitimate demands of the working class. Batista's dictatorship grew more hated the longer it was in existence, and, although he became a profound embarrassment for the United States, the American government continued to support his regime until the last. Only Fidel Castro dared to oppose the Batista dictatorship.

MONCADA BARRACKS Soon after Batista's seizure of power, Fidel Castro began making plans for a revolution. Slowly he started to acquire arms and recruited followers from the ranks of recent university graduates. By the summer of 1953 he had acquired 165 followers (plus 2 women who also joined his revolutionary band). All of them were under thirty years of age, and most of them were university graduates who came from urban, middle class families. Castro's heart and soul was wrapped up in his revolution, and he was able to inspire in his followers a fanatical loyalty to his cause and his leadership. He made them believe that they were fighting for a better life for the Cuban people, and undoubtedly Fidel Castro was sincere in his intentions. His immediate plans were to attack the Moncada army barracks in Santiago de Cuba, seize control of that city, and mobilize popular discontent with Batista as a power base from which the rest of Oriente Province could be liberated from his dictatorship. Once the rebels were in control of Oriente Province it would be simply a matter of time before they were in control of all of Cuba. In a manifesto issued just before the attack on the Moncada Barracks, Fidel Castro pledged to liberate Cuba from foreign economic control, subtly appealing to Cuban resentment of the United States, promised to implement land reform to reduce the economic power of the *latifundistas*, vowed to improve the lot of Cuba's industrial workers, and, finally, called for the establishment of political democracy in Cuba. Unfortunately, the attack on the Moncada Barracks did not go as planned.

FIASCO Castro's rebel band gathered at a chicken farm near Siboney on the outskirts of Santiago. They were to break up into two attack forces and strike the Moncada Barracks from two different directions. Half of the attack force became lost in the unfamiliar streets of Santiago, were unable to find the army barracks, and were not on hand when they were most needed in the heat of battle. The other half of the attack force was unlucky enough to stumble across an armed patrol just as they were about to attack, and the patrol was able to warn the Moncada Barracks that an attack was coming. Virtually all of Castro's force was captured, and half of his men were to die under army torture. Only the frantic intervention of the archbishop of Santiago

saved the rest of the rebel force from a similar fate.
Castro, himself, was able to escape the scene of battle,
but became the object of an intensive manhunt. On August 1, 1953, an army patrol under the command of Lt.
Pedro Suares, a Negro officer, captured Castro while
he was asleep in the hut of a friendly peasant. Fortunately for Castro, Lt. Suares was a humane man and
instead of returning him to the Moncada Barracks,
where he almost certainly would have been tortured to
death, he turned him over to civil authorities in Santiago de Cuba. In September, 1953, Castro went on trial
for treason; in October he was sentenced to 15 years
imprisonment in the penal colony on the Isle of Pines.
THE 26TH OF JULY MOVEMENT Castro spent the
next twenty-two months (four months in solitary confinement) in prison on the Isle of Pines, and during
that period Mirta divorced him. However, his imprisonment was not uneventful. He read voraciously
and absorbed a wide variety of political works, including the writings of Marx and Lenin, which he
seems to have come upon for the first time. According to Matthews, Castro's reading of Marx and Lenin
was superficial, and they did not register much of an
impression on him. Later, Castro would claim that
he moved closer to Marxism-Leninism while in prison. In any event, Castro wrote a justification of his attack on the Moncada Barracks entitled *History Will
Absolve Me*, and he managed to smuggle the pamphlet
out of jail by writing it (with lemon juice which became
visible only when the paper was heated with a hot iron)
between the lines of routine letters to his family and
friends. The letters were carefully collected by his
associates, pieced together, and published in the hopes
of arousing support for the revolutionary movement.
Castro called his group the 26th of July Movement
(the date of the attack on the Moncada Barracks),
and promised free elections, free press, free speech,
an independent judiciary, military disarmament, and
restoration of the Constitution of 1940. Castro has yet
to implement a single promise made to the Cuban people in *History Will Absolve Me*. On May 15, 1955,
Batista, feeling that Castro had been rendered harm-

less and hoping to improve his tarnished reputation in the United States, amnestied Fidel Castro and released him from the Isle of Pines. It was the most catastrophic mistake Fulgencio Batista ever made.

ON TO MEXICO No sooner was Castro out of jail than he announced the formation of his revolutionary organization, which he described as an "organization of the humble, by the humble and for the humble." He called upon all Cubans to join his "struggle of the people," but the response to his appeal was less than overwhelming. Making his way back to Havana, Castro worked as a journalist and attacked the Batista regime in the pages of *La Calle.* He succeeded only in getting the paper closed down by the authorities, and he was banned from the Cuban radio. Realizing that he was getting nowhere in Cuba and despairing of toppling Batista from within, he left for Mexico in July, 1955, hoping to launch an expedition from there which would overthrow the Batista regime. The Mexican government kept a close watch on Castro and his activities, for it is a violation of international law for one country to allow its territory to be used as a base of attack against a neighboring state with which it is at peace. Mexico has its own laws against Communist agitation, but since Fidel Castro stoutly denied that he was a Communist or a Communist sympathizer, and since he had no connections with known Communists, he was not arrested by the Mexican police.

THE *GRANMA* EXPEDITION In October, 1955, Fidel Castro toured the Cuban communities in New York City, Philadelphia, and Miami, trying to raise funds for his planned expedition against Cuba. Returning to Mexico, Castro was joined by Ernesto "Che" Guevara, an Argentine medical doctor and adventurer, and by his brother Raoul, in addition to other Cuban exiles. In 1956 he began laying up arms in preparation for his attack on Batista, but the Mexican police constantly raided his hideouts and seized his weapons. It was all Castro could do to find places secure from the raids of the Mexican authorities. Finally, he managed to collect a respectable stock of weapons, and he purchased the *Granma,* a beat-up yacht designed to carry a dozen

14

people, as the carrier of his expedition. This time, Castro worked out a realistic plan of operations. Frank Pais, the leader of the Fidelistas in Oriente Province, was to stage an armed insurrection against the Batista regime on November 30, 1956, and join forces with Castro when the *Granma* arrived. Simultaneously, the 26th of July Movement would call upon the Cuban people to support the rebels by going out on a general strike, which hopefully would paralyze the economy and prevent Batista's military machine from operating effectively. Had Castro's plan gone off as scheduled, Batista might well have been toppled. But again, the *Granma* expedition turned out to be a comedy of errors. On November 25, 1956, Castro and 81 followers jammed themselves onto the *Granma* and sailed towards Cuba. Instead of arriving on November 30th, as planned, the *Granma* did not reach Cuba until December 2nd. Frank Pais began his insurrection as scheduled, but Castro was not there to meet him, and the uprising in Oriente Province was easily suppressed. The general strike never developed, and Batista was warned of Castro's arrival on the *Granma*. On December 5, 1956, Castro's 82 man force was intercepted by Batista's army at Alegria de Pio, and, after an intense fight, Castro's expedition was smashed to bits. Those who managed to survive (reckoned at about a dozen men) fled to the safety of the Sierra Maestra Mountains. When the survivors succeeded in re-establishing contact with their fellow rebels, it was found that they had only seven rifles among them. Disheartened and disspirited, it seemed that the Granma survivors and the 26th of July Movement were both finished. A joyous Fulgencio Batista claimed that Fidel Castro had been killed in battle, and not until two months later did the world learn differently.

THE SPIRIT OF THE SIERRA MAESTRA Fidel Castro was not disillusioned. True, he had suffered his second major setback in as many attempts to overthrow Batista, but he was convinced that history was on his side and that eventually his cause would triumph. He communicated his spirit of optimism to his small band of followers, and soon they were also believing that they would inevitably triumph and were vowing to continue the fight. Without being aware that he was doing so, Castro decided to adopt the tactics of guerrilla warfare made famous by Mao Tse-tung. He decided to harass the Batista forces in hit-and-run raids until he was strong enough to launch a general offensive. The raids would serve the dual purpose of replenishing Castro's supply of arms and munitions and would demonstrate the vulnerability of the Batista regime. Hopefully a series of successful raids would increase the general discontent with Batista and attract new followers for the 26th of July Movement. Castro quickly won the support of the Sierra Maestra peasants, who aided his men in order to show their resentment against their landlords. It is highly unlikely that the rebels could have survived without the aid of the peasants, and it is to them that Castro owes the success of his revolution. In February, 1957, the Resistencia Civica was organized in Santiago de Cuba as the urban guerrilla arm of the Fidelista movement. It was to do in the cities what Castro was doing in the mountains, but, for the most part, the urban guerrilla movement proved ineffectual and it was in the Sierra Maestra that the revolution was really won.

THE MANUFACTURE OF A HERO In February, 1957, Herbert L. Matthews, a reporter for the New York *Times,* succeeded in making contact with Castro's guerrillas, and the sensational dispatches which he filed for the *Times* were instrumental in turning Fidel Castro into a popular hero. Realizing that favorable international publicity would immeasurably aid his cause, Fidel Castro was determined to make a favorable impression on Matthews and treated him like visiting royalty. At the time, Castro had exactly 18 men under his command, but he convinced Matthews that he was actually commanding a far larger force, and that it was making significant gains against Batista. He spent hours with Matthews, telling him of his hopes and aspirations for Cuba, and convincing him that he was leading a democratic movement. "It is a revolutionary movement," Matthews concluded, "that calls itself socialistic. It is also nationalistic, which generally in Latin America means anti-Yankee. The program is vague and couched in generalities, but it amounts to a new deal for Cuba, radical, democratic and therefore anti-Communist.'' Matthews' photos of the young, bearded revolutionaries made a favorable impression on the American public, and Castro's men became romantic symbols of democratic freedom fighters entitled to the sympathy of all free men. The romantic image of Castro was reinforced in April, 1957, when a CBS news crew presented a highly laudatory documentary on the Fidelistas on American television. When Castro finally seized power in Cuba, he had behind him a huge reservoir of American goodwill. The pity of it is that he failed to make good use of that American goodwill.

GROWING STRENGTH On March 13, 1957, students at the University of Havana stormed the Presidential Palace in an attempt to assassinate Fulgencio Batista. The *coup* failed miserably and resulted in heavy loss of student life, but it did demonstrate the intensity of the domestic opposition to Batista and the appeal of the Fidelista movement. In May the entire nation was stunned (and Batista severely humiliated) when Judge Manuel Urrutia broke with his other two colleagues and voted to acquit 100 surviving rebels of the November, 1956, Santiago uprising on the grounds that they had a constitutional right to rebel against the tyranny of the Batista regime! That same month, Fidel Castro scored his first significant military victory over Batista when his forces successfully attacked the El Uvero army barracks and captured large stocks of arms. After El Uvero Cubans began to flock to Castro's banner, and within the span of a year his forces grew from a few score men to a substantial army of 3000 guerrilla fighters. By August, 1957, Fidel Castro was dominant in the Sierra Maestra Mountains, and the authority of the Havana government ended where the mountains began. In September the Cuban navy staged an insurrection at the Cienfuegos naval base, and though Batista's army and air force crushed the insurrection, it marked the first time that a portion of the Cuban military establishment had rebelled against the regime. At this point the United States government should have seen the handwriting on the wall and cut off its support of the Batista government. Unfortunately, Ambassador Earl E.T. Smith could not see the obvious, and on his advice the Eisenhower administration continued its support of Batista, thus encouraging the justifiable wrath of Cuban nationalists.

VICTORY In March, 1958, Fidel Castro sent his brother Raoul with 53 men to open a second front against Batista in the Sierra de Cristal on the eastern end of the island. As the rebels gained strength, the United States belatedly cut off arms shipments to Batista that March, but incredibly Eisenhower permitted American military experts to go on advising and training Batista's army! On April 9, 1958, Castro called upon the Cuban people to begin a general strike to force Batista's resignation from office. However, the leaders of the Cuban labor unions were all henchmen of Batista, who were using union funds to fatten their own pockets, and they managed to stifle the strike which failed miserably. But the Cuban Communists, who saw that Batista's days were numbered, offered their support to Castro. Unwilling to turn down the support of any Cuban group and seeking to create a truly national revolutionary movement, Castro accepted their support and made his first contact with the Communist party. On May 24th Batista launched a massive and all-out offensive in the Sierra Maestra Mountains designed to wipe out the guerrillas once and for all time. For a while Castro's men were hard pressed, but the pressure was relieved in June when the Fidelistas won a major victory over Batista's lackluster army at Santo Domingo. The Cuban army had little love for Batista and still less desire to kill their fellow Cubans in order to keep him in power. After Santo Domingo the will of the Cuban army to fight was shattered, and by mid-August the Sierra Maestra offensive was acknowledged to be a shambles. Still the Eisenhower administration doggedly continued to support Batista!

CLOSING BATTLES In the fall of 1958 the Fidelistas went on the offensive. By early November, Castro's forces were on the outskirts of Santiago de Cuba, and

Oriente Province was soon in their possession. On December 29th Batista's forces were routed at Santa Clara, and the dictator realized that it was all over. He did not wait for the rebel army to reach Havana. Instead, he fled the country early on New Year's Day. At thirty-two years of age Fidel Castro was master of Cuba, and on January 8, 1959, he rode into Havana astride an army tank, amid the cheers of the populace. He appeared reluctant to assume power directly, and instead Manuel Urrutia, the judge who had refused to convict the Santiago rebels, was proclaimed president of the provisional government, and Miro Cardona, an anti-Batista politician, became premier. Although Urrutia and Cardona were the nominal heads of the Cuban government, they soon discovered that Fidel Castro, as leader of the Rebel Army, was the man who actually wielded power in Cuba. Why Castro went through the charade of installing a civilian government is not known.

That January, just days after Castro's final victory over Batista, Herbert L. Matthews again interviewed him for the New York *Times*. During the course of their conversation the elderly Matthews, who had seen many revolutions, warned Castro that he held enormous power which could be used for evil as well as good. Looking incredulous, Castro replied in a puzzled tone, "But how could *I* do harm?" The statement reveals much about Castro's psychological make-up and helps to explain why his revolution embraced despotism instead of democracy. Like other leftist leaders around the world, Fidel Castro has deceived himself into believing that only he knows what is best for his people and that all his actions are dedicated to their best interests. When his policies do not bring results as fast as he would like, or when his policies meet opposition, Castro ascribes moral evil and degeneracy to his critics and opponents. Since he is well-meaning, everything he does is noble and good; whereas his opponents are corrupt and self-seeking. Consequently, Castro's suppression of the opposition (in his own mind) is not an act of tyranny, but a fulfillment of the people's will. Since his opponents frustrate the will of the people (and of Castro), they forfeit all their democratic rights and can have no claim on society or on Castro. Accordingly, Fidel Castro's concept of democracy is very much different from the American conception of democracy; his concept does not allow for dissent from the will of the people (which he embodies) and becomes a totalitarian democracy in which no one may dissent from the majority will as he defines it.

THE COMMUNIST TAKE-OVER OF CUBA On February 16, 1959, Fidel Castro ended the pretense of civilian control of the Cuban government by ousting Miro Cardona as premier and assuming the office himself. He would spend the next fourteen months consolidating his power, purging democratic officials from their positions, and installing Communists in their place. The first modern leader to govern by television, Castro became famous for his frequent harangues (which often lasted five or six hours) to the Cuban people in which he made grandiose promises which were impossible of fulfillment. For example, on the day he became premier, he asserted, "I am sure that in a few years we will raise the Cuban standard of living above that of the United States." The statement revealed Castro's total lack of knowledge of the problems facing Cuba or the difficulties involved in economic modernization. When he could not make his promise come true, he blamed Cuba's plight on his favorite whipping boy, the United States. In any event, that spring Castro shocked the American people by the glee which he took in the public execution of some 600 alleged "war criminals" who were executed after being found guilty in trials which appeared to be a mockery of justice. The entire officer corps of the regular Cuban army was discharged and replaced by veterans of Castro's Rebel Army; the regular Cuban police was replaced by a Communist dominated revolutionary police which became an instrument of repression; and a vast peasant militia was created by the Fidelistas and taught to hate Yankee Imperialism and to regard the United States as their mortal enemy.

THE RUIN OF THE MIDDLE CLASS In May, 1959, Castro proclaimed an Agrarian Reform Law which

proved to be disastrous for Cuba. The large plantations (including those owned by American corporations)
were seized by the state and turned into peasant com-
munes, and all land rents were slashed by 50%. The
result of the Agrarian Reform Law was to wipe out
middle class farmers and drive them off the land. The
peasants who took over the farms and plantations lacked
the skills necessary for efficient agricultural produc-
tion, and the Cuban economy was soon in a shambles.
By 1962 the sugar harvest fell 1,000,000 tons short of
the government's expectations, and such food staples as
rice, beans, meat, chickens, fish, eggs, milk, and pota-
toes had to be strictly rationed by the state in order to
ward off mass hunger and starvation. Castro's own
mother and sister fled Cuba, denounced his mismanagement of the economy, and joined the anti-Castro
Cuban community in exile. Confiscation of the plantations and farms was followed by the expropriation of
some $800 million worth of American investments in
Cuba. Under international law such expropriations are
legal, provided the owners of the seized properties
are compensated at a fair market value. To this day the
Communist dictator of Cuba has refused to pay a single
cent to American investors and denounces the United
States government for daring to demand compensation
for American business interests. In July, 1959, Castro
went on television to announce that if Manuel Urrutia
did not resign the presidency, then he would resign
as premier. Urrutia had denounced the increasing in-
fluence of the Communists in the government, and
Castro feared that he might become the leader of an
anti-Castro opposition. The Cuban people shouted their
love for Fidel by screaming for Urrutia's blood. The
hapless president resigned his office and fled the country. He was soon joined by Manuel Ray, Minister of
Public Works, and Rufo Lopez-Fresquet, Minister of
the Treasury, as well as a growing host of other dedicated Cuban officials.
INTERNATIONAL MENACE "The duty of every revolutionary," Fidel Castro has declared, "is to make
revolution." Having triumphed in Cuba, Castro was
determined to export his revolution and subvert the

21

other Latin American republics. In April, 1959, he outfitted an expedition designed to topple the government of Panama; in June, he sought to foment revolution in the Dominican Republic; and in August Haiti became the target of his imperialistic designs. While all these expeditions failed, they revealed Castro's determination to war upon his neighbors. In January, 1962, the Organization of American States unanimously voted its condemnation of Castro's international "banditry," and since 1964, no Latin American nation (until Communist Chile resumed relations with Cuba in 1971) has traded with Cuba, and only Mexico has continued to maintain diplomatic relations with Castro's government.

INTERNAL OPPOSITION In the ten years from 1959 to 1969 an estimated 300,000 to 500,000 (1 Cuban in 16) people have fled Fidel Castro's Communist tyranny for the United States and other Latin American nations. An additional 400,000 people are presently awaiting their turn to leave Castro's Cuba! In order to be able to leave Cuba, these refugees must surrender all their property and wealth to the state, which not only enriches the Castro regime but also eliminates much of the domestic opposition to his rule. However, back in 1959 and 1960, a counter-revolutionary guerrilla movement was organized in the Sierra de Escambray Mountains and in Las Villas and Pinar del Rio provinces. The anti-Castro guerrillas hoped to gain the support of the United States and hoped that America would permit anti-Castro exiles to outfit an expedition against Cuba from the United States. In June, 1959, Major Pedro Diaz Lanz, head of the Cuban Air Force, defected to the United States and warned against the dangers of a Communist take-over of the island. When Major Diaz later dropped anti-Castro leaflets over Havana, Castro violently denounced the United States. The Eisenhower administration watched Castro with growing alarm. Instead of establishing freedom of the press and speech, Castro severely punished all criticism. In December, 1959, Major Hubert Matos, Commander of the Rebel Army in Camaguey Province and a member of Castro's original guerrilla band, was sentenced to twenty years imprisonment for warning against Communist penetration of the Cuban government. Finally, in February, 1960, Anastas Mikoyan opened a Soviet trade mission in Havana and gave Castro a $100 million loan plus the promise of huge arms shipments. Eisenhower decided it was time to act.

TOWARDS THE BAY OF PIGS In March of 1960 President Eisenhower approved the Central Intelligence Agency's supplying and training of a Cuban exile invasion force. Under the leadership of Manuel Artime, the exiles were trained in Guatemala and Nicaragua, and were outfitted with American weapons. This was a serious breach of international law, but was justified by the United States on the grounds that Fidel Castro was a menace to the peace and security of the Western Hemisphere and that the sooner he was overthrown, the better it would be for all concerned. Hoping that economic sanctions might bring the Cuban dictator to reason, the United States in July, 1960, suspended the Cuban sugar quota (it refused to buy any more Cuban sugar). Castro was not chastened. He responded by continuing his expropriations of American businesses in Cuba, and on August 7th the U. S. State Department issued a white paper documenting its contention that Castro had deliberately undermined U.S.-Cuban relations, had betrayed his democratic promises, and had permitted Communists to take control of his government. That same month diplomatic relations between the United States and Cuba were suspended. In September, Nikita Khrushchev and Fidel Castro came to New York to attend the fall meeting of the United Nations General Assembly. Staying at a hotel in Harlem, Castro's party kept live chickens in their suite and turned their rooms into pigstyes. At the U.N. he accused the United States of promoting aggression against Cuba and charged that the Central Intelligent Agency was committing acts of sabotage and guerrilla warfare inside Cuba. In January, 1961, diplomatic relations between the United States and Cuba were permanently broken off, and President John F. Kennedy, agreeing with Eisenhower's estimation of

Castro's danger to American security, decided to go ahead with the planned invasion of Cuba.

THE BAY OF PIGS On April 16, 1961, two American B-26's based in Nicaragua and flown by CIA agents were shot down by Soviet supplied Cuban jet fighters. The B-26's were to have been given an escort of American jet fighters based on the carrier *Essex*, lying in international waters off the Cuban coast. Unfortunately, the jet fighters arrived at their rendezvous point an hour before the slower B-26's, and when the bombers finally arrived they were shot down before they were able to complete their mission. It was an omen of the fiasco to follow. That night, Fidel Castro went on Cuban television and announced that his government was now dedicated to the promotion of a socialist revolution and that Cuba was now a member of the Marxist-Leninist bloc of nations. At 2:00 A.M. the next morning a 1400 man force of Cuban exiles stormed ashore at the Bay of Pigs. The counterrevolution was underway.

Hoping to destroy the Cuban Air Force, bombers based on Guatemala bombed the Havana airport, but Castro was expecting such an attack and dispersed his air force. A Russian T-33 bomber sighted and sank the *Houston,* the expedition's ammunition and communications ship, at the start of the invasion. The anticipated rising of the Cuban people against the Castro regime failed to materialize, and the Cuban militia slowed the advance of the exile force until the army could be mobilized. The exiles were stranded on Cuba and running short of ammunition and supplies. Only the active military intervention of the United States could save them, but President Kennedy refused to employ American armed forces to salvage the invasion. On April 19th, out of ammunition and with no hope of reinforcements, the 1100 plus survivors of the Bay of Pigs landing surrendered to the Cuban army. Castro used the national emergency created by the invasion to justify his arrest of 200,000 suspected revolutionaries, and the internal anti-Castro guerrilla movement was destroyed. The failure of the Bay of Pigs invasion eliminated all opposition of Castro's regime and firmly committed him to Marxism-Leninism. That June a Cu-

24

ban secret police was created with the help of Russian advisors, and the hapless survivors of the expedition had to be ransomed by the United States for $53 million worth of food and medicines.

"I AM A MARXIST-LENINIST" On the night of December 1-2, 1961 Fidel Castro again harangued the Cuban people on television. This time he told them that he had been a Marxist-Leninist ever since he was a student at the University of Havana and that he had always intended to lead Cuba down the path towards socialism. If Castro is to be taken at his word, it means that all his previous statements about establishing a democratic political order in Cuba were deliberate and premeditated lies. Matthews claims that Castro made the statement in order to reinforce Soviet support for his regime, that he genuinely feared an American invasion of his island nation, and that he felt that a frank avowal of Marxism-Leninism would make it impossible for Russia to permit him to be overthrown by the United States. In any event, he closed his speech by declaring, "I am a Marxist-Leninist and I shall be a Marxist-Leninist until the last day of my life." In order to consolidate his hold over Cuba's political life, Fidel Castro created the Integrated Revolutionary Organization which was a coalition of his 26th of July Movement, the old Cuban Communist party, and various other radical groups. It was the only legal political party in Cuba, and to make certain that his authority would not be challenged, Castro, in March, 1962, purged Anibal Escalants and his followers. Escalante was the long-time head of the old Cuban Communist party, and the demotion of his followers meant that Castro was the sole source of political power in Cuba. It was also a warning to Moscow that he would not be upstaged by the old-line Communists and that he would be the master of the Cuban Communist party.

THE CUBAN MISSILE CRISIS Since the Bay of Pigs invasion, the United States government estimates that the Soviet Union has been pouring $1 million per day into Castro's Cuba, and that other Iron Curtain countries are contributing another $300,000 worth of aid per day to Cuba. Today, Cuba is the most heavily armed nation in Latin America, and the vast quantities of Soviet bloc economic aid is the only thing saving the Cuban economy from complete collapse. Sometime in 1962 Fidel Castro, in dread of an American invasion which he believed to be imminent, asked Nikita Khrushchev to install nuclear missiles in Cuba to shield him against an American military attack. During the summer, Raoul Castro went to Moscow to work out the final details. It was agreed that the missile sites were to be manned by the Russians and under their complete control. SAM-2 missiles (short range anti-aircraft rockets) as well as intermediate range ballistic missiles (capable of hitting cities along the Atlantic seacoast and in the American Mid-West) would be secretly installed in Cuba. Castro would have his nuclear umbrella, and the Soviet Union would dramatically alter the world balance of power by establishing a military beachhead in the Western Hemisphere and by putting American cities under the threat of nuclear attack from a base only ninety miles from Florida. Had the Russians been able to complete their installation without being detected by the United States, they would have presented America with a *fait accompli* which could not have been reversed without the threat of nuclear devastation to American cities. Fortunately, on October 14, 1962, a U-2 spy plane discovered the missile sites before the Russians had had time to make them operational.

CASTRO'S HUMILIATION Fully supported by every single member of the Organization of American States, President Kennedy announced that the United States Navy would quarantine Cuba and prevent all ships from reaching the island until such time as Premier Khrushchev withdrew his missiles from the island. Behind the scenes, President Kennedy made it crystal clear that if the missiles were not speedily withdrawn, the United States was prepared to invade Cuba and topple the Castro regime. For thirteen fateful days the crisis raged, and during all that time Fidel Castro was ignored. He had to endure the humiliation of sitting by helplessly while the United States and Russia settled the fate of his nation. Finally, on October 28th, without even consulting Castro, Khrushchev indicated that he would immediately pull his missiles out of Cuba and agreed to United Nations inspection of the missile sites to insure their complete dismantlement. Fidel Castro was hopping mad and refused to permit U.N. inspection of Cuba. President Kennedy did not insist upon U.N. inspection, declaring that aerial reconnaissance was a sufficient check on Castro, and he assured Premier Khrushchev that the United States would not use military force to topple the Castro regime. Fidel Castro had been publicly humiliated and deserted by his Russian allies when he needed them the most; however, he was so heavily dependent on Russian economic aid that he could do nothing except swallow his anger. In the spring of 1963 Castro was invited to visit the Soviet Union so that amends could be made for his earlier humiliation. Ironically, the missile crisis rallied Cuban public opinion behind Castro. Cuba faced the imminent threat of a United States invasion if the missiles were not removed, and Castro, acting as the defender of the nation, was able to employ the latent anti-Americanism of the Cuban people to his advantage.

THE AFTERMATH Since the missile crisis, the United States has reconciled itself to a Communist Cuba, and though Castro claims that the CIA is still conducting sabotage raids against his nation, there have been no attempts to topple his regime by force of arms. Castro, however, has repeatedly displeased the Soviet Union by trying to foment revolutions in Venezuela, Brazil, Costa Rica, Puerto Rico, Chile and Bolivia (where his top aide, "Che" Guevara, was killed in October, 1967). Moscow opposes this policy since it fears United States intervention in Latin America. If a Communist revolution is suppressed by the Americans, it would damage Russia's international prestige; if the U.S. permitted another Communist revolution to succeed in Latin America, Russia would be obligated to extend economic aid and it can barely afford to support the Cuban Communists, let alone others. Fortunately, Castro has not succeeded in exporting his revolution, and he is presiding over a Cuba in economic disarray.

THE CONTINUING FAILURE OF CUBAN AGRICUL-
TURE In August, 1962, the Castro regime admitted
that the 1959 Agrarian Reform Law was a failure
and that the Cuban people had not responded favor-
ably to the attempt to establish collective farms.
In October, 1963, Castro enacted the 2nd Agrarian Reform Law which expropriated every farm over
165 acres and which placed all sugar cultivation
under state control. Thirty percent of Cuba's farm-
land remains in private ownership, but all farmers
must grow what the state tells them to and must sell
their produce at the government's price. With all economic incentives destroyed, Cuban agriculture has
fared badly, and important food staples are still being
strictly rationed. The failure of the sugar crop (Cuba's
chief export commodity) has been especially notable.
The 1968 sugar harvest was one million tons under the
1967 harvest, and the 1969 crop fell 3.5 million tons
short of Castro's goal for the year. Peasants have been
so reluctant to work for the state that since 1963, the
army and so-called urban volunteers have been mobilized to harvest the cane. The urban volunteers are
government workers and university students who cannot afford to antagonize the regime.

URBAN CONDITIONS The dismal failure of Cuban
agriculture has been mirrored by the failure of industry to meet the needs of the Cuban people. The
Central Planning Board, headed by Fidel Castro, has
overall charge of the Cuban economy and has been
attempting to develop and diversify industry. However,
this effort has been severely retarded by the exodus
of the highly skilled Cuban middle class and by the
gross mismanagement of the Castro regime. Such
everyday items as soap, toothpaste, electric light
bulbs, matches, and household detergents are often
unobtainable at any price; and televisions, radios,
automobiles, and refrigerators are priced so high as
to be beyond the reach of 99% of the Cuban people.
Theoretically, every Cuban family is guaranteed rent-
free apartments. However, urban housing is in such
short supply that five or six families are forced to
share facilities designed for two or three families, so

that slum conditions quickly become general. In the countryside, the vast majority of the people still live in thatched huts without running water or electricity. Because there are so few consumer goods available for purchase, Cuba has suffered from runaway inflation which the government has tried to combat by implementing a program of forced savings. Unfortunately, forced savings often appear confiscatory to workers and depresses productivity by destroying incentive. In March, 1968, Castro outlawed all private businesses, street vendors, and independent artisans as counterrevolutionary. He has insisted upon state control of all business activity, but has succeeded only in producing an equality of misery. As an authority on Cuba glumly concluded, "Castro promised bread and freedom; he brought austerity and totalitarianism."

PLUS AND MINUS Castro's administration of Cuba has not been all bad. He has succeeded in banishing corruption from the government, and his is the first honest government (in the sense that public officials are no longer diverting public funds to their own personal bank accounts) that Cuba has ever had. The national lottery has been purged of corruption; American criminals no longer control Havana gambling casinos (which have been closed down); and prostitution has been banished from the streets of Cuba's cities. Crime in Havana has been sharply reduced, and it is safer to walk the streets of Havana at night than it is to walk the streets of New York City in broad daylight. Every Cuban child is attending school (along with more than 1 million adults) and receives wholesome meals provided by the state. The Castro administration has cut the rate of illiteracy from 27% to 3% of the population in less than a decade. Unfortunately, the quality of Cuban education is extremely low because most of Cuba's best teachers have fled the country. Their place has been taken by inexperienced young Communist ideologues, and propaganda forms the core of the Cuban school curriculum. Children are taught to hate the United States and to regard Yankee Imperialism as Cuba's greatest enemy. While all Roman Catholic schools and universities have been taken over by the state, and while Spanish-born priests have been expelled from the country, Castro, unlike the other Communist leaders, has made no attempt to impede the free exercise of religious worship. All churches remain open, and the Cuban people are free to attend them without official harassment. However, like other Communist lands, Cuba has made free thought a crime against the state. In 1964 the regime acknowledged that it was holding 15,000 political prisoners (most of them peasants who resisted Castro's agrarian program), and a year later it admitted that that figure had risen to 20,000 and was still climbing (on a percentile basis it would be the equivalent of 600,000 Americans imprisoned for their political beliefs). Outside sources put the number of political prisoners at a much higher figure. Their only crime is their publicly expressed lack of faith in the Castro regime, and they are being reeducated (brainwashed) to see the error of their ways and to fit into Castro's Communist society.

THE MAXIMUM LEADER As Prime Minister, Secretary General of the Communist Party of Cuba (reorganized in 1965 as the only legal party in Cuba), and Commander-in-Chief of the Armed Forces, Fidel Castro is the undisputed master of Cuba. In 1966 Rolando Cubelas, supported by the CIA and exile leader Manuel Artime, unsuccessfully attempted to assassinate Castro in Havana; and, in January, 1968, Castro purged the last of the oldline pro-Moscow Communists in the Cuban party. Today, Fidel Castro is supreme in Cuba, and he has succeeded in eliminating all opposition to his rule. He has yet to implement any of the democratic promises he made between 1953 and 1959. Under his leadership, Cuba threw off its dependency upon the United States only to become even more dependent upon the Soviet Union. It has lost a half-million of its most educated and able citizenry (with untold economic consequences), and, except for Canada and Chile, it is without a friend in the Western Hemisphere. Castro has failed to improve or to modernize the Cuban economy, he has failed to materially improve the lot of the Cuban masses, and there appears to be no chance of his abandoning Communism. Why he took Cuba down the Communist road is still not fully known. Obviously, he believed that Communism would enable Cuba to modernize and resolve her problems much faster than a continuation of the free enterprise system would. In that guess he was wrong, and the great tragedy of his career is his betrayal of the hopes and aspirations of the Cuban people for a better life in a democratic society.

SamHar Press

Division of Story House Corp.

BIBLIOGRAPHY

BY CASTRO: Two useful collections of Castro's speeches and writings are: *History Will Absolve Me* (1959); and *Fidel Castro Speaks*, ed. by Martin Kenner & James Petras (1970).

BIOGRAPHIES: The best full-length biography is Herbert L. Matthews, *Fidel Castro* (1969). Jules Dubois' *Fidel Castro* (1959) is badly outdated. Rufo Lopez-Fresquet's, *My Fourteen Months with Castro* (1966) is a useful first person memoir.

PRO-CASTRO ACCOUNTS: Favorable accounts of Castro and the Cuban revolution abound, but should be used with the utmost caution because they are trying to promote a particular ideological persuasion. The more important pro-Castro works are: Edward Boorstein, *The Economic Transformation of Cuba* (1968); Regis Debray, *Revolution in the Revolution* (1967); Les Huberman and Paul M. Sweezy, *Cuba, Anatomy of a Revolution* (1961), and *Socialism in Cuba* (1969); C. Wright Mills, *Listen Yankee* (1960); Elizabeth Sutherland, *Cuba Now!* (1967); and Robert Taber, *M-26: Biography of a Revolution* (1961).

ANTI-CASTRO ACCOUNTS: Generally more accurate than the pro-Castro accounts, the anti-Castro works should also be used cautiously for they are also promoting an ideological persuasion. The leading anti-Castro works are: Teresa Casuso (a one-time associate of Castro), *Cuba and Castro* (1961); Warren Miller, *Ninety Miles from Home* (1961); and Manuel Urrutia Lleo, *Fidel Castro and Co., Inc.: Communist Tyranny in Cuba* (1964).

SCHOLARLY TREATMENTS: The standard works on Castro's Cuba are Theodore Draper's *Castroism: Theory and Practice* (1965), and *Castro's Revolution: Myths and Realities* (1968). Other sound studies are: Boris Goldenberg, *The Cuban Revolution and Latin America* (1965); Wyatt MacGaffey and Clifford R. Barnett, *Twentieth Century Cuba: The Background of the Castro Revolution* (1965); John Plank (ed.), *Cuba and the United States* (1967); Ramon Eduardo Ruiz, *Cuba, the Making of a Revolution* (1968); Robert Scheer and Maurice Zeitlin, *Cuba: An American Tragedy* (1964); Dudley Seers, *Cuba: The Economic and Social Revolution* (1964); Robert F. Smith, *The United States and Cuba: Business and Diplomacy, 1917–1960; What Happened in Cuba?: A Documentary History* (1963), and *Background to Revolution: The Development of Modern Cuba* (1966); Lester A. Sobel (ed.), *Cuba, the U.S. and Russia, 1960–63* (1964); Andre Suarez, *Cuba: Castroism and Communism, 1959–1966* (1967); Jose Yglesias, *In the Fist of the Revolution: Life in a Cuban Country Town* (1969); and Maurice Zeitlin, *Revolutionary Politics and the Cuban Working Class* (1967).

SPECIAL SUBJECTS: Hugh Thomas' definitive *Cuba: The Pursuit of Freedom* (1970) is an excellent history of the island which is useful in placing Castro within proper historical perspective. For the Cuban missile crisis and U.S.-Cuban relations see: Elie Abel, *The Missile Crisis* (1966); Roger Hilsman, *To Move a Nation: The Politics of Foreign Policy in the Administration of John F. Kennedy* (1967); Robert F. Kennedy, *Thirteen Days* (1970); and Arthur M. Schlesinger, Jr., *A Thousand Days* (1965). On the Bay of Pigs fiasco consult: Haynes Johnson, et. al., *The Bay of Pigs*(1964); Karl E. Meyer and Tad Szulc, *The Cuban Invasion: The Chronicle of a Disaster* (1962). Excellent journalistic accounts of Castro's Cuba are: Herbert L. Matthews, *The Cuban Story* (1961), and *Cuba* (1964); and Lee Lockwood's *Castro's Cuba, Cuba's Fidel* (1969). Richard R. Fagen, et. al. discuss the refugee problem in *Cubans in Exile* (1968).